110309
S.
3.95

FIGURE SKATING

THE STORY OF CANADIANS IN THE OLYMPIC WINTER GAMES

Written by Blaine Wiseman

Weigl

Published by Weigl Educational Publishers Limited
6325 10 Street SE
Calgary, Alberta
T2H 2Z9

www.weigl.com

Library and Archives Canada Cataloguing in Publication data available upon request.
Fax 403-233-7769 for the attention of the Publishing Records department.

ISBN 978-1-55388-942-7 (hard cover)
ISBN 978-1-55388-951-9 (soft cover)

Printed in the United States of America
1 2 3 4 5 6 7 8 9 0 13 12 11 10 09

Editor: Heather C. Hudak
Design: Terry Paulhus

All of the Internet URLs given in the book were valid at the time of publication. However, due to the dynamic nature of the Internet, some
addresses may have changed, or sites may have ceased to exist since publication. While the author and publisher regret any inconvenience
this may cause readers, no responsibility for any such changes can be accepted by either the author or the publisher.

Every reasonable effort has been made to trace ownership and to obtain permission to reprint copyright material. The publishers would be
pleased to have any errors or omissions brought to their attention so that they may be corrected in subsequent printings.

Weigl acknowledges Getty Images as its primary image supplier for this title.

We gratefully acknowledge the financial support of the Government of Canada through the Book Publishing Industry Development Program
(BPIDP) for our publishing activities.

Contents

4 What are the Winter Olympics?

6 Canadian Olympic Figure Skating

8 All the Right Equipment

10 Qualifying to Compete

12 Rules of Figure Skating

14 Exploring the Venue

16 Illustrating Figure Skating

18 Olympic Legends

20 Olympic Stars

22 A Day in the Life of an Olympic Athlete

24 Olympic Volunteers

26 What are the Paralympics?

28 Olympics and the Environment

30 Creating Choreography

31 Further Research

32 Glossary/Index

What are the Winter Olympics?

The Olympic Games began more than 2,000 years ago in the town of Olympia in Ancient Greece. The Olympics were held every four years in August or September and were a showcase of **amateur** athletic talent. The games continued until 393 AD, when they were stopped by the Roman emperor.

The Olympics were not held again for more than 1,500 years. In 1896, the first modern Olympics took place in Athens, Greece. The games were the idea of Baron Pierre de Coubertin of France. Though they did not feature any winter sports, in later years, sports such as ice skating and ice hockey were played at the Olympics.

In 1924, the first Olympic Winter Games were held at Chamonix, France. The Games featured 16 nations, including Canada, the United States, Finland, France, and Norway. There were 258 athletes competing in 16 events, which included skiing, ice hockey, speed skating, and figure skating.

Today, there are several figure skating events featured in the Winter Olympics. There are individual events in both men's and women's competitions, as well as pairs and ice dancing events that feature teams of one man and one woman skating together. Some of the top figure skating nations are Canada, the United States, Russia, France, Japan, Germany, and China.

TOP 10 MEDAL-WINNING COUNTRIES

COUNTRY	MEDALS
Norway	280
United States	216
USSR	194
Austria	185
Germany	158
Finland	151
Canada	119
Sweden	118
Switzerland	118
Democratic Republic of Germany	110

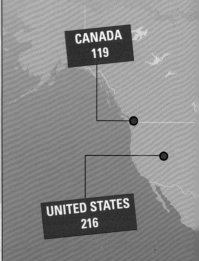

CANADA 119

UNITED STATES 216

🍁 **CANADIAN TIDBIT** Vancouver will be the third Canadian city to host the Olympic Games. Montreal hosted the Summer Games in 1976, and Calgary hosted the Winter Games in 1988.

Winter Olympic Sports

Currently, there are seven Olympic winter sports, with a total of 15 **disciplines**. All 15 disciplines are listed here. In addition, there are five Paralympic Sports. These are alpine skiing, cross-country skiing, **biathlon**, ice sledge hockey, and wheelchair curling.

Alpine Skiing

Biathlon

Bobsleigh

Cross-Country Skiing

Curling

Figure Skating

Freestyle Skiing

Ice Hockey

Luge

Nordic Combined

Short Track Speed Skating

Skeleton

Ski Jumping

Snowboarding

Speed Skating

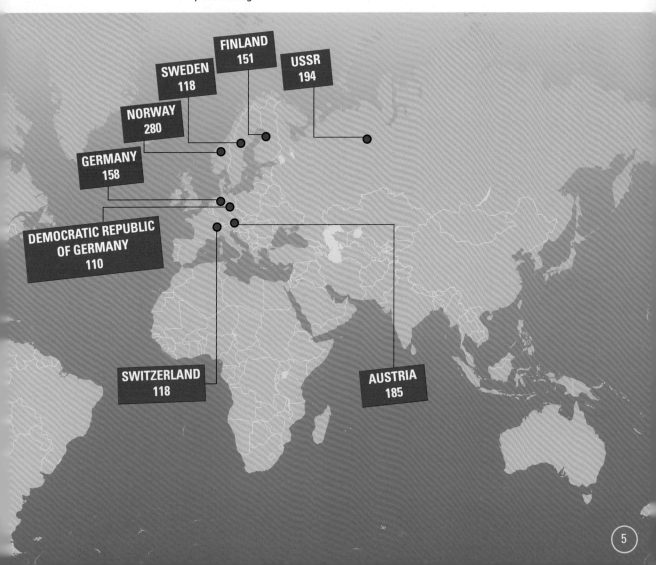

FINLAND
151

SWEDEN
118

USSR
194

NORWAY
280

GERMANY
158

DEMOCRATIC REPUBLIC
OF GERMANY
110

SWITZERLAND
118

AUSTRIA
185

Canadian Olympic Figure Skating

In Montreal in 1887, figure skater Louis Rubenstein formed the first national Canadian skating association. Rubenstein was the first Canadian figure skating champion. He was so skilled that, when he won a Russian tournament in 1890, he was named "Champion of the Universe."

Canada named Elizabeth Manley its athlete of the year in 1988.

Canada won its first Olympic figure skating medals in 1932 at Lake Placid, New York. Montgomery Wilson finished in third place in the men's competition, winning the bronze medal. In 1948, Barbara Ann Scott won Canada's first Olympic figure skating gold medal. At the same Olympics, Suzanne Morrow and Wallace Distelmeyer won the bronze medal in the pairs event. Morrow and Distelmeyer gained fame that year by performing the first **death spiral**, a move that has become one of the most recognizable in pairs figure skating.

Canada's next figure skating medal came eight years later, when Frances Dafoe and Norris Bowden won silver in the pairs competition in 1956. At the following Olympics, in 1960, the Canadian pair of Barbara Wagner and Robert Paul won a gold medal, while Donald Jackson won a bronze medal in the men's event. It was 12 years before Canada won another figure skating medal. At the 1972 Olympics, Karen Magnussen won silver. Four years later, Toller Cranston won a bronze medal in the men's event. Then, Brian Orser won silver in 1984.

Barbara Ann Scott was known as "Canada's Sweetheart." Not only was Scott the first Canadian to win an Olympic gold medal in figure skating, but she was also the first non-European to win a world championship.

Elvis Stojko beat out Kurt Browning at the 1994 Canadian Figure Skating Championships, winning his first national title in figure skating.

In 2002, Salé and Pelletier became the first non-Russian figure-skating pair to win Olympic gold in 42 years.

At the 1988 Winter Olympics in Calgary, Alberta, Canadians won more figure skating medals than at any previous Olympics. Brian Orser and Elizabeth Manley each won silver medals in individual competitions, while Tracy Wilson and Robert McCall won bronze in ice dancing, Canada's first medal in that event.

Isabelle Brasseur and Lloyd Eisler won a bronze medal in the pairs event at the following Olympics, and they won their second straight bronze medal in 1994. This was the same year that Elvis Stojko won his first world championship title soon after winning a silver medal at the Olympics at the 1994 Olympics in Lillehammer.

In the final skate of the pairs event in 2002, Jamie Salé and David Pelletier skated perfectly, while their Russian opponents committed a few errors. When the judges gave their results, the Russian team was declared the winner and awarded the gold medal, surprising many people. Later, one of the judges admitted that she had been told to vote for the Russians instead of the Canadians. After several days, the International Olympic Committee (IOC) decided that Jamie Sale and David Pelletier should also be awarded a gold medal. This was Canada's second gold medal for the pairs event, and it came 42 years after the first.

🍁 **CANADIAN TIDBIT** Jeffrey Buttle won a bronze medal in men's figure skating at the 2006 Olympics.

All the Right Equipment

The most important piece of equipment required for figure skating is a pair of ice skates. Figure skates are designed to help skaters complete spins on the ice and launch themselves into the air to perform **aerial** stunts.

The first known ice skates developed thousands of years ago in Scandinavia. These simple devices were made from a piece of bone that was attached to the bottom of a sandal. In the 18th century, wealthy Europeans began combining skating and dancing. They used skates made from wood for this early form of figure skating. Later, metal blades were attached to winter boots.

Today's figure skates consist of leather boots that have metal blades attached to the bottom. At the front of the skate blade, there is a toe pick that has a series of teeth. These teeth dig into the ice so that the skater can spin at high speeds. Digging the toe pick into the ice also can help the figure skater gain more power for jumping.

Another important piece of equipment for figure skaters is their costume. Figure skating is a performance sport in which skaters must impress the judges with their skill and appearance. Each skater wears a different costume for his or her performance at the Olympics and other competitions. The costumes that skaters wear for competitions are usually brightly coloured and unique. Tassels and sparkles are common aspects of figure skating costumes.

SKATES ---

Figure skaters have their elaborate costumes custom designed by professionals.

Skaters wear elaborate costumes that blend with the music they choose for their performance, creating a theme. For example, a male skater who chooses an Elvis Presley theme might slick his hair and wear a leather jacket while skating to the song *Hound Dog*. A female who uses the theme of *The Nutcracker* might wear a ballerina outfit while Tchaikovsky's music plays on the speakers.

Figure skate blades are longer than hockey skate blades and shorter than speed skate blades.

BLADES

❖ **CANADIAN TIDBIT** Canadian figure-skating legend Elvis Stojko often wore costumes that reflected his personality. At the Olympics in 1994, Stojko wore a martial-arts-style costume while performing a Kung Fu-themed program that was inspired by Bruce Lee.

Qualifying to Compete

Jessica Dubé and Bryce Davison finished second in the pairs competition at the HomeSense Skate Canada International in Ottawa, on November 1, 2008.

Reaching the Olympics is a difficult task for a figure skater. A skater must complete several criteria before he or she will be allowed to compete as an Olympian.

There are only a certain number of spots available for each figure skating competition. In the individual events, there are 30 spots for men and 30 spots for women. There are spots for 20 pairs teams and 24 ice dancing teams. Every country is allowed three spots in each event. This means that if four Canadian women qualify for the individual women's event, the top three qualifiers are usually sent to the Olympics.

The first step to qualifying for the national team is by competing in national championships. The second step is to compete in and perform well at international competitions. The top-placing 24 men, 24 women, 19 dancing couples, and 16 pairs at the World Figure Skating Championships the year before the winter Olympics automatically qualify. The remaining spots are filled at another international competition.

Qualifying for the Olympics takes a great deal of dedication and hard work. There is tremendous pressure on skaters to perform well at qualifying events. All of a skater's training and hard work are put to the test at these events.

At the 2006 Winter Olympics, Americans Tanith Belbin and Benjamin Agosto won silver in the ice dancing competition.

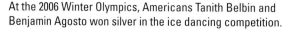

At the 2002 Olympics, judges allowed Marie-France Dubreuil and Patrice Lauzon to restart their routine when Marie-France's costume became entangled in Patrice's shirt.

JUDGING

After the situation involving Jamie Salé and David Pelletier in 2002, a new system of judging was introduced. The technical panel is made up of five people who ensure that the judges are grading the competition in a fair and proper manner. The technical specialist identifies each element of the performance and assigns it a level of difficulty. Twelve judges watch the competition and give each competitor marks on his or her performance. Judges grade each element according to how well the skater executes them. This is called the Grade of Execution (GOE).

Skaters are also judged on skating skills, **transition**, performance, **choreography**, and **interpretation**. Each of these components are graded on a scale of 1 to 10. The judge's final score, called the segment score, is a combination of the GOE and the component score. Although all 12 judges mark the skater, only nine of the judge's scores are used to calculate a skater's final score. The nine judges are chosen in a random draw before the performance. At the end of each skater's performance, nine segment scores are added together to give the skater's final score.

Rules of Figure Skating

Figure skating is a very competitive sport that requires skill, rhythm, and passion. One slip can mean the difference between victory and disappointment. Skaters must incorporate certain elements and components into each routine if they want to achieve Olympic success.

The men's and women's individual events consist of two performances for each skater. These are called the short program and the free skate. Women's and men's short program performances cannot be longer than two minutes and 50 seconds. In the women's competition, the free skate can be as long as four minutes, while the men's can be four minutes and 30 seconds. The free skate is worth more points than the short program, and must show creativity, innovation, and a high level of difficulty. Each skater must combine spins, footwork, and jumps in his or her programs.

The pairs event features teams of one woman and one man skating together. Each pair performs a short program and a free skate that include a series of tricks, including throws, spins, and lifts, as well as synchronized jumps, spirals, and steps.

Ice dancing features couples moving together in a mix of skating and ballroom dancing. Instead of overhead lifts and jumps, couples perform **synchronized** steps and dance moves, while staying in contact with the ice for most of the performance. Olympic ice dancing consists of three performances for each couple. These are the **compulsory** dance, original dance, and free dance.

Olympic figure skaters must follow certain rules in each event if they want to perform a successful routine and impress the judges.

For the compulsory dance, each couple must perform the same routine. They are judged on how well they **execute** the dance. There are many factors that judges watch for when comparing couples. Small differences in the performances can make a big difference in the final score.

The original dance has a set pattern, but each team can interpret this pattern in its own way. The free skate gives the teams the most freedom. Creativity is an important part of the free skate. There is no set pattern for performance, and couples design their own routine.

Successful pairs skaters know how to communicate well and listen to each other.

PERFORMANCE ENHANCING DRUGS

Although the Olympics are a celebration of excellence and sportsmanship, some athletes use performance enhancing drugs to give them an unfair advantage over other athletes. There are many different types of performance enhancing drugs, including steroids. Some make muscles bigger, others help muscles recover more quickly, while some can make athletes feel less pain, giving them more **endurance**. The International Olympic Committee (IOC) takes the use of performance enhancing drugs very seriously. Regular testing of athletes helps ensure competitors do not use drugs to unnaturally improve their skills. Figure skating requires a mixture of strength, speed, and endurance. Many performance-enhancing drugs will help an athlete in one of these areas, but hurt them in others. For example, a drug may cause the heart to pump more blood to muscles in the arms, making the athlete physically stronger. This takes blood away from the heart and lungs, giving the athlete less endurance and slower long-term recovery. There are serious mental and physical health problems that arise from using these drugs, such as sleep problems, sickness, and high blood pressure. Athletes who use steroids for a long time may die early from heart attacks and other problems.

Exploring the Venue

Canadian fans cheered when the 2010 Olympic torch was unveiled for the first time.

Olympic events are held in huge, specially built venues around the host city. These buildings can be used to exhibit one or multiple events, and can cost more than $1 billion to build.

Thousands of people attend figure skating events, so the Olympic venue must hold a large number of spectators. In 2010, Olympic figure skating events will be held at the Pacific Coliseum in Vancouver, British Columbia. The Pacific Coliseum has been used in the past for NHL hockey games, concerts, fairs, and many other large events.

CEREMONIES

Two of the most-anticipated and popular events of the Olympics are the opening and closing ceremonies. These events are traditionally held in the largest venue that an Olympic host city can offer. Facilities such as football, baseball, or soccer stadiums are often used for these events. At the 2008 Olympic Games in Beijing, more than 90,000 people attended the opening ceremonies. The ceremonies are spectacular displays that

include music, dancing, acrobatic stunts, and fireworks. The theme of the ceremonies usually celebrates the history and culture of the host nation and city. All of the athletes participating

in the Olympics march into the stadium during the ceremonies. The athletes wave their country's flag and celebrate the achievement of competing in the Olympics.

Upgrading the Pacific Coliseum cost the government of Canada and British Columbia millions of dollars.

For the Olympics, the building received more than $20 million in renovations. It will also be used for the Olympic short track speed skating events.

Figure skating competitions take place on an international-sized ice rink. The ice surface at the Pacific Coliseum was originally built to host NHL hockey games, which are played on a smaller ice surface than is required for Olympic figure skating. As a result, the ice surface had to be made larger. The dimensions of the rink are 64 metres long by 30 metres feet wide. There are no lines or circles on a figure skating rink. Skaters can travel across the entire rink during their performance.

Other renovations to the venue included adding new washrooms and concessions, and installing a new ice plant, which keeps the ice surface frozen. The building has been updated to accommodate 14,239 spectators. The old seats from the arena were sold at an auction to raise money for Vancouver sports.

The Coliseum is home to the Vancouver Giants junior hockey team.

🍁 **CANADIAN TIDBIT** The Olympic Stadium in Montreal is one of the most expensive stadiums ever built, costing more than $1.4 billion.

Illustrating Figure Skating

THE DEATH-DROP SPIN

Probably the most spectacular, this is a flying camel spin landing in a back sit spin. The skater jumps off the outside front foot and lands in a sitting position on the right foot.

REFEREE
Among other things, he is responsible for eligibility of officials, skaters, and the jury; allocating ordinal ranks from the scores; and resolving disputes.

ASSISTANT REFEREE
He assists the referee and replaces him if necessary.

TIMEKEEPER
The routine times are predetermined, and he makes sure that these times are respected.

JUDGES

ISU TECHNICAL DELEGATES (2)
They make sure that the technical facilities meet ISU standards.

THE TOE LOOP

The toe loop is the simplest of the toe pick jumps. The skater takes off facing backward.

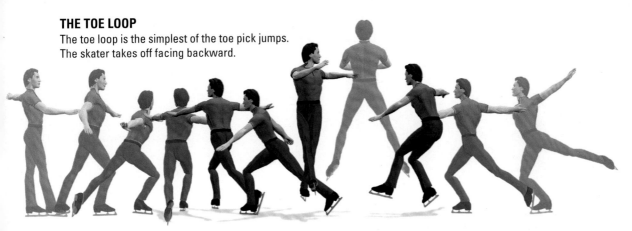

CALCULATION OF MARKS

Since 1988, the judges for international competitions have been drawn by lot from among the represented nations. This system is in force in the European and world championships. Two sets of marks on a scale of 0 to 6, the first for technical execution and the second for artistic presentation, are awarded by 9 judges. A list of deductions is given to the judges before each event. In addition to the basic marking scale, this list provides the judges with more accurate evaluation standards. Thus, for example, a poorly performed step sequence is penalized by 0.1 to 0.3 of a mark; poorly performed combinations, spins, or jumps cost 0.1 to 0.4 of a point, and an element not skated costs 0.5 of a point.

JUDGES
They come from the participating countries, and most are ex-skaters. Each event has different judges.

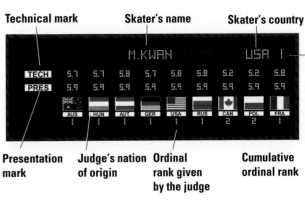

Technical mark · Skater's name · Skater's country

Presentation mark · Judge's nation of origin · Ordinal rank given by the judge · Cumulative ordinal rank

TECHNICAL AND PRESENTATION SCORING SCALE

0: not skated
1: very poor
2: poor
3: mediocre
4: good
5: very good
6: perfect

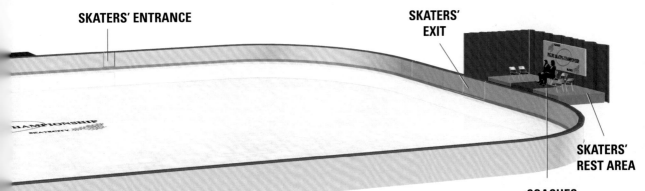

SKATERS' ENTRANCE

SKATERS' EXIT

SKATERS' REST AREA

COACHES
They give final advice before the performance.

Olympic Legends

FAST FACT

Scott was the first woman to land a figure skating move called a double **lutz** in competition.

OLYMPIC MEDALS WON

1 Gold

Barbara Ann Scott

Known as "Canada's Sweetheart," Barbara Ann Scott won Canada's first-ever Olympic figure skating gold medal. At the age of nine, Scott began training for seven hours every day. She won the 1940 Canadian Junior Championships and soon moved into senior competition.

Scott dominated women's figure skating throughout the mid-1940s. In 1944, she won her first Canadian Championship and kept the title through 1948.

She was also the North American champion from 1945 through 1948 and won the European Championship in 1947 and 1948. The night before the women's 1948 Olympic figure skating competition in St. Moritz, Switzerland, the ice hockey gold medal had been won by Canada. The hockey game left the ice full of ruts and snow. Organizers tried repairing the ice, but the weather was warm, and the ice turned to slush. Despite the conditions, Scott skated a perfect performance, winning the gold medal. Scott was so popular that after the Olympics, a Barbara Ann Scott doll was sold across Canada.

FAST FACT

Stojko is a three-time Canadian Kung Fu champion. He combined the art of Kung Fu with figure skating to create his unique style on the ice.

OLYMPIC MEDALS WON

2 Silver

Elvis Stojko

Although Elvis Stojko never won a gold medal at the Olympics, he is remembered as one of the greatest figure skaters in history for his electric Olympic performances. Stojko's unique style made him a fan favourite. In 1994, Stojko won the Canadian Championships and the World Championships with his famous Bruce-Lee-themed performance. At the Olympics that year, Stojko narrowly came in second place.

Although many people disagreed with the judges' decision, Stojko accepted the medal with grace. Stojko trained hard and dominated the figure skating circuit for the next four years. In 1998, he recorded a perfect performance at the Canadian Championships, only one month before the Olympics.

Five days before the men's competition at the Olympics, Stojko caught a serious case of the flu. Fighting through his illness, he continued preparing for the event. Only eight hours before the event, Stojko pulled his groin. Although he could barely walk, he decided to compete. Despite being sick and injured, Stojko won the silver medal.

Jamie Salé and David Pelletier

In 2002, the Canadian pairs team of Jamie Salé and David Pelletier became global celebrities when they won Canada's first figure skating gold medal in more than 40 years. Salé and Pelletier, who are married, began skating together in 1998.

The couple won their first Canadian Championship in 2000 and held the title in 2001 and 2002. In 2001, they also won the World Championship, after finishing in fourth place the year before. However, Salé and Pelletier are best known for their 2002 Olympic gold medal in pairs figure skating. Salé and Pelletier's almost perfect performance in the free skate portion of the competition came immediately after Salé was injured in a collision with Anton Sikharulidze of Russia in the warmup. Staying positive and being the best figure skating pair in the world made Salé and Pelletier Olympic legends.

FAST FACT

A new judging system was implemented for figure skating due to Salé and Pelletier's controversial win at the 2002 Olympics.

OLYMPIC MEDALS WON

1 Gold

Sonja Henie

Norway's Sonja Henie was only 11 years old when she competed in the first Winter Olympics in 1924. Two years later, Henie came in second place at the World Championships. In 1928, at 15, she won her first Olympic gold medal. She won two more gold medals at the 1932 and 1936 Olympics.

Henie was only 23 years old when she won her third straight Olympic gold medal. One week after winning gold at the 1936 Winter Olympics, Henie won her 10th straight World Championship. To this day, no other skater has won 10 World Championships.

Henie was so popular that she toured the world during the 1930s. Huge crowds would come to see her, and police would have to keep the crowds under control. When her skating career was over, Henie appeared in two movies. They were called *Thin Ice* and *Sun Valley Serenade*.

FAST FACT

Henie was a third-ranking female tennis player in Norway.

OLYMPIC MEDALS WON

3 Gold

Learn about competitive figure skating at **http://entertainment.howstuffworks.com/competitive-figure-skating.htm**.

Figure skating news can be found by visiting **www.ctvolympics.ca/figure-skating/index.html?cid=navtsn**.

Olympic Stars

Patrick Chan

Patrick Chan trains in Toronto, Ontario. In 2007, Chan finished in second place at the World Junior Championships. The following year, he moved into senior competition.

At his first World Championships, Chan finished in ninth place. He improved over the next year and came in second place at the 2009 World Championships, establishing himself as one of the top skaters in the world. He finished in first place at the 2008 and 2009 Canadian Championships.

OLYMPIC MEDALS WON

1 Gold   1 Silver

Evgeni Plushenko

Russia's Evgeni Plushenko is the best-known men's figure skater in the 2010 Olympics. Plushenko wanted to be an Olympic champion since he was four years old. He won his first World Championship in 2001 and competed in his first Olympics in 2002. At the Olympics, Plushenko was disappointed when he won the silver medal. He again won the World Championships in 2003 and 2004.

Plushenko was in top form entering the Olympics in 2006, and he hoped that he could reach his goal of winning an Olympic gold medal. He put on the performance of a lifetime, beating the silver medalist by a record score of 27 points.

Joannie Rochette

At the 2006 Winter Olympics, in Turin, Italy, Joannie Rochette came very close to winning a medal for Canada. Finishing in fifth place, Rochette was the highest-placing Canadian in figure skating that year.

Rochette first competed on the senior figure skating circuit in 2002. That year, she finished in third place at the Canadian National Championships.

At the next two Canadian Championships, she improved her result, finishing in second place. In 2005, Rochette won the Canadian Championship and has held the title every year since. In 2008, Rochette had her best finish at the World Championships, coming in fifth place, but beat that result in 2009 by finishing in second place.

Jessica Dubé and Bryce Davison

Although both Jessica Dubé and Bryce Davison compete in individual figure skating events, it is in the pairs event that they have had their greatest success.

In 2006, Dubé and Davison had a very successful year. In their first Winter Olympics performance, they finished in 10th place. That same year, the couple placed second at the Canadian Championships and seventh at the World Championships.

The following year, they won their first Canadian pairs championship and again placed seventh at the World Championships. At the 2008 World Championships, Dubé and Davison finished in third place, winning the bronze medal.

WANT MORE?

For current figure-skating news, check out **www.cbc.ca/sports/figureskating**.

Learn more about figure skating in Canada at **www.skatecanada.ca**.

A Day in the Life of an Olympic Athlete

Becoming an Olympic athlete takes a great deal of dedication and **perseverance**. Athletes must concentrate on remaining healthy and maximizing their strength and energy. Eating special foods according to a strict schedule, taking vitamins, waking up early to train and practise, and going to bed at a reasonable hour are important parts of staying in shape for world-class athletes. All athletes have different routines and training regimens. These regimens are suited to that athlete's body and lifestyle.

Eggs are a great source of **protein** and **iron**, and are low in **calories**, making them a popular breakfast choice. A cup of orange juice is a healthy breakfast drink, while coffee can give an athlete some extra energy in the morning. A light lunch, including a sandwich, yogurt, fruit, and juice, is usually a good option. This gives the body the right amount of energy, while it is not too filling. Chicken and pasta are popular dinnertime meals.

Between the months of July and December, skaters spend most of their time training on the ice.

Early Mornings

Olympic athletes might wake up at 6:30 a.m. to record their resting **heart rate**. Next, they might stretch or perform yoga while their breakfast is being prepared. The first exercise of the day can happen before 7:00 a.m. Depending on an athlete's sport, the exercise routine can vary. A skater might be in the gym lifting weights with their legs. After lifting weights for an hour, the athlete may move on to **aerobics** to help with strength and endurance.

6:30 a.m.

Morning Practice

By about 9:30 a.m., athletes are ready to practise their events. For a figure skater, this means lacing up the skates and hitting the ice. After practice, skaters stretch to keep their muscles loose and avoid injuries. Many athletes use a sauna or an ice bath to help their muscles recover quickly.

9:30 a.m.

Afternoon Nap

At about noon, many athletes choose to take a break. Sleep helps the body and mind recover from stress. After waking up more exercise. **Core** exercises help figure skaters with stability. They use special workout equipment to exercise their core. Speed and quickness exercises are important for figure skaters. A common exercise for foot speed is to quickly move the feet through a course on the ground. The course can be as simple as a few sticks laid on the floor.

12:00 p.m.

Dinnertime

After the afternoon workout, it is dinnertime. Another healthy meal helps athletes recover from the day, and prepares their bodies for the next day's training. The evening can be spent relaxing and doing some more light stretches. It is important for athletes to rest after a hard day of training so that they can do their challenging routine again the next day.

6:00 p.m.

Olympic Volunteers

Rain or shine, Olympic volunteers work to make sure the Olympics run smoothly.

To keep the Games running on track, volunteers use snowblowers to clear outdoor race courses.

Volunteers are an important part of creating an enjoyable Olympic experience for athletes and spectators. Thousands of volunteers help organize and execute the Olympic Games. Olympic volunteers are enthusiastic, committed, and dedicated to helping welcome the world to the host city. Volunteers help prepare for the Olympics in the years leading up to the events and even after the Olympics are over.

Before the Olympics begin, many countries send representatives to the host city to view event venues and plans. Olympic volunteers help make the representatives' stay enjoyable. From meeting these representatives at the airport, showing them around the city and the surrounding areas, and providing accommodations and **transportation**, volunteers make life easier for visitors to the host city.

🍁 **CANADIAN TIDBIT** About 25,000 volunteers are helping with the Olympics in Vancouver. They are helping to make sure that the games are a memorable, enjoyable experience for athletes, judges, spectators, and officials from all over the world.

During the Olympics, volunteers help in many different areas. In the opening, closing, and medal ceremonies, volunteers help with the costumes, props, and performers. Editorial volunteers help by preparing written materials for use in promoting events and on the official website of the Olympic host. Food and beverage volunteers provide catering services to athletes, judges, officials, spectators, and media personnel.

Some volunteers get a chance to view events and work with competitors. Anti-doping volunteers notify athletes when they have been selected for drug testing. These volunteers explain the process to the athletes and escort them to the drug-testing facility. Other volunteers become involved with the sporting events by helping to maintain the venues and the fields of play, providing medical assistance to athletes, transporting athletes to events, and helping with the set-up and effective running of events.

The Olympic torch is lit at the ancient site of Olympia by robed women who use curved mirrors to ignite the flame using the Sun. It is then carried to the host city by volunteer torch bearers.

TORCH RELAY

One of the most anticipated events of each Olympics is the torch relay. The torch is lit during a ritual in Olympia, Greece, before it is flown to the host nation. The torch is then carried along a route across the country, until it reaches the host city during the opening ceremonies. The torch relay for 2010 covers 45,000 kilometres over 106 days. For the 2010 Olympics, the relay will begin in Victoria before moving through communities in all 10 Canadian provinces and three territories. About 12,000 volunteers will be chosen to carry the torch across Canada. Other volunteers help drive and maintain the vehicles that accompany the torch on its journey.

What are the Paralympics?

First held in 1960, the Paralympic Games are a sports competition for disabled competitors. The games, like the Olympics, celebrate the athletic achievements of the competitors. The Paralympics are held in the same year and city as the Olympics and feature summer and winter competitions. Many sports appear in both the Paralympics and the Olympics, such as swimming, nordic skiing, and alpine skiing. The Paralympics also feature wheelchair basketball, **goalball**, and ice sledge hockey. The first Winter Paralympic Games were held in 1976.

Athletes competing at the Paralympics are classified by disability in six categories, including **amputee**, **cerebral palsy**, **visual impairment**, **spinal cord** injuries, **intellectual disability**, and a group of other disabilities. These groups let organizers put athletes on even footing for most events. Goalball, for example, is a sport for the visually impaired, not for amputees.

Ice sledge hockey is traditionally a men's sport. However, women will be allowed to compete for the first time in ice sledge hockey at the 2010 Olympics.

The Paralympics hold their own opening and closing ceremonies that are similar to the Olympics.

To turn the sit-ski, skiers lean in the direction they want to turn as they drag their ski pole in the snow.

Some Paralympic sports use specially adapted equipment. Ice sledge hockey is a sport for people with disabled legs. Players sit on a special sled, or sledge, with two blades on the bottom side that allow the puck to pass underneath. Players use two small hockey sticks to push themselves along the ice and to handle the puck. One end of the stick has a blade like a regular hockey stick, and the other end has a spike. The blade end is used to handle the puck, and the players dig the spike into the ice to propel themselves around the rink. Alpine skiers have specially built ski poles with small skis on the bottom. This sport is for people who have had a leg amputated. Skiers use the poles to help push them along, as well as to balance them.

The sit-ski was one of the first skis developed for athletes using wheelchairs.

Olympics and the Environment

Hosting so many people in one city can be costly to the environment. Host cities often build new venues and roads to accommodate the Games. For example, a great deal of transportation is needed to support construction projects, planning for the games, and to move the athletes, participants, volunteers, media, and spectators around the host city and its surrounding areas. This transportation causes pollution.

In recent years, the IOC and Olympic host cities have been working to make the Olympics more green. With their beautiful surroundings, including the Pacific Ocean to the West and the Rocky Mountains to the East, Vancouver and Whistler have taken many steps to protect the environment.

Vancouver is known around the world for its sustainability programs.

WHISTLER SLIDING CENTRE

At the Whistler Sliding Centre, home to the bobsleigh, luge, and skeleton events, an ice plant is used to keep the ice frozen. The heat waste from this plant is used to heat other buildings in the area. All wood waste from the Whistler sites will be chipped, composted, and reused on the same site.

LIL'WAT ABORIGINAL NATION

Working with the Lil'wat Aboriginal Nation, builders of the Olympic cross-country ski trails created venues that could be used long after the Olympics. About 50 kilometres of trails have been built that can be used by cross-country skiers and hikers of all skill levels.

VANCOUVER LIGHTING AND HEATING SYSTEMS

Venues in Whistler and Vancouver have been equipped with efficient lighting and heating systems. These systems reduce the amount of **greenhouse gases** released into the atmosphere during the Olympics.

GREENHOUSE GASES

Half of the organizing committee's vehicles are either **hybrid** or equipped with fuel management technology. These vehicles emit less greenhouse gases than other vehicles. As well, venues have been made accessible to users of transit, and many event tickets include transit tickets to promote mass transportation at the games.

VANCOUVER CONVENTION AND EXHIBITION CENTRE

The Vancouver Convention and Exhibition Centre uses a seawater heating system. This system uses the surrounding natural resources to make the building a more comfortable place to visit. The centre also houses a fish habitat.

RICHMOND OLYMPIC OVAL

The Richmond Olympic Oval was built with a wooden arced ceiling. The huge amount of wood needed to build the ceiling was reclaimed from forests that have been destroyed by mountain pine beetles. These beetles feed on pine trees, killing them in the process. Using this wood helps stop other, healthy trees from being cut down for construction materials.

🍁 **CANADIAN TIDBIT** The 2010 Games are estimated to cost more than $4 billion, including about $2.5 billion of taxpayer money.

Creating Choreography

Aside from maintaining top physical condition, figure skaters must also learn to dance a choreographed routine. Figure skating is a sport that tests artistic, as well as athletic, ability. The best skaters are creative and able to incorporate their own personality into their routines.

Try choreographing a dance performance to show your friends, parents, or teacher.

What you need

Music player and music
a large, open space

1. Pick a song to which you want to dance. Figure skating routines use many different types of music. From opera to rock to hip hop, any song that you choose can be used to create a routine.

2. Remember that figure skaters must make use of certain moves in their routine. Include jumps, spins, and fancy footwork in your performance.

3. When you are choreographing your routine, try to make the moves match the music. If the beat or sound of the music becomes louder or faster at a certain point, you can perform a spinning jump. During slower parts, a slow spin might be better.

4. Figure skating routines always end with a special pose in the centre of the ice. Practise your routine so that you know the order of your moves, and you can finish with a pose at the end of the song.

5. Try drawing a costume design that matches the music you chose.

6. Perform your routine for friends or family.

Further Research

Visit Your Library

Many books and websites provide information on figure skating. To learn more about figure skating, borrow books from the library, or surf the Internet.

Most libraries have computers that connect to a database when searching for information. If you input a topic, you will be provided with a list of books in the library that contain information on that topic. Nonfiction books are arranged numerically, using their call number. Fiction books are organized alphabetically by the author's last name.

Surf the Web

Learn more about figure skating by visiting **www.olympic.org/uk/sports/programme/history _uk.asp?DiscCode=FS&sportCode=SK**.

To learn all about the Olympics in 2010, visit **www.vancouver2010.com**.

Glossary

aerial: occurring in the air

aerobics: exercise for the heart and lungs

amateur: an athlete who does not receive money for competing

amputee: a person who has had a part of his or her body removed

biathlon: a sport in which athletes combine cross-country skiing and target shooting skills

calories: units of energy in food

cerebral palsy: a condition that typically causes impaired muscle coordination

choreography: the planning of a skating routine

compulsory: another word for required or necessary

core: the trunk of the body, including the hips and torso

death spiral: a technique used in pairs skating in which the male spins in a circle, staying in one place on the ice, while holding the hand of his female partner, who also spins in a circle around him

disciplines: subdivisions within a sport that require different skills, training, or equipment

endurance: the ability to continue doing something that is difficult

execute: another word for perform

goalball: a sport for blind athletes that has bells inside the ball

greenhouse gases: gases that are trapped within Earth's atmosphere by the greenhouse effect

heart rate: the number of times the heart beats in one minute

hybrid: a vehicle that uses a combination of fuels

intellectual disability: a disability that hampers the function of the mind

interpretation: making a routine fit well with the musical selection

iron: a substance in foods that is good for the blood

lutz: a jump in figure skating in which the skater makes a 360-degree turn between taking off from the back outer edge of one skate and landing on the back outer edge of another skate

perseverance: a commitment to doing a task despite challenges that arise in the process

protein: substance in food that keeps body tissues healthy

spinal cord: a bundle of nerves held inside the spine, connecting almost all parts of the body to the brain

synchronized: occurred at the same time

transition: moving smoothly from one move to the next

transportation: the use of vehicles to move people

visual impairment: not being able to see well

Index

blade 8, 9, 27

Calgary 4, 7
Chan, Patrick 20
costume 8, 9, 11, 25, 30

Davison, Bryce 10, 21
Dubé, Jessica 10, 21

Henie, Sonja 19

judging 7, 8, 11, 12, 13, 18, 19, 24, 25

Pelletier, David 7, 11, 19
Plushenko, Evgeni 20

Rochette, Joannie 21

Salé, Jamie 7, 11, 19
Scott, Barbara Ann 6, 18
spin 8, 12, 30
Stojko, Elvis 7, 9, 18

torch 14, 25

Vancouver 4, 14, 15, 24, 28, 29
volunteer 24, 25, 28